Humanism for Parents

Parenting without Religion

By

Sean P. Curley

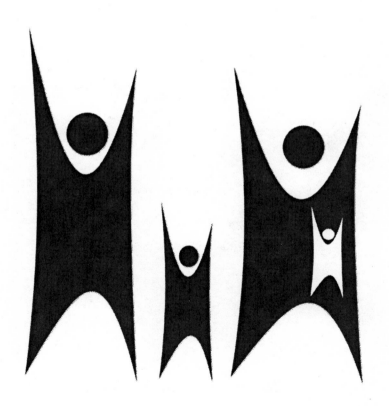

Published by Lulu

Copyright © 2007 Sean P. Curley

First publication 2007

www.lulu.com

www.spiritualhumanist.info

humanismforparents@spiritualhumanist.info

ISBN: 978-1-4303-1425-7

Portions of this book were previously published on

http://spiritualhumanist.info and
http://spiritualhumanist.blogspot.info

Printed in the United States of America

Contents

For Humanist Parents Everywhere

Special thanks to:
Jenny Fox for insightful input and many hours spent reviewing;
my children Ryan, Tamair, Caitlin, & Seamus for letting us practice;
and Darcie Curley for putting up with me.

Introduction

Parenting has always been difficult and modern times are no exception. Historically, parents have had religious rites, rituals, and practices to rely on. People who want to parent without this reliance on religion, whether or not they are themselves religious, struggle with these missing elements. This book is an overview of parenting with Humanism, or parenting without the influence of the historical practices of religion. It is a practical guide that is meant to address the differences encountered in non-religious parenting.

People frequently misunderstand Humanism, primarily because it is such a general philosophy and encompasses many of the non-religious as well as mildly religious practices. The first chapter therefore discusses Humanism, at least from my perspective. If you want to gain a general understanding of Humanism, read this chapter.

One of the most common mistakes about a Humanist, or more specifically – an Atheist, is that they can't be *moral* because religion is required to define moral behavior. This is patently false and the second chapter discusses this in some depth. Religion as the basis of morality is a common argument from religious people. Unless you are very comfortable with the concept of morality without religion, you should read this chapter.

Chapter III is a short guide to common sense good parenting. These tenets of good parenting are common between religious and non-religious families. Of course, many people have very different views on exactly what good parenting is and this is just one opinion, so take it as that and nothing more. If you want a refresher on basic good parenting principles, then read this chapter.

Chapter IV is the heart of the book and includes various sections on specific topics about parenting and Humanism; don't skip this chapter or you shouldn't have purchased this book!

With the *New Atheism* (a more radical and revolutionary stance on religion) from the likes of Sam Harris and Richard Dawkins, there is a lot of discussion about the dangers of religion. This is especially prevalent in the United States of America who some are now calling a *Christian Nation*. Chapter V discusses this looming cultural war along with how it might affect you and your family. Any parent trying to raise non-religious children should read this chapter.

Chapters VI and VII are for you to either read to your children or have them read. I attempted to write these chapters at an appropriate reading level for your children. Of course, reading levels vary significantly from person to person. Even though I tried to keep the language age-appropriate, you may need to interpret some of the answers.

Finally, there is the question of just how to apply Humanism to contemporary moral issues. Chapter VIII is the most contentious and controversial and is the one that will not stand up to the test of time. It is also the most subjective as it must include personal opinions and beliefs. You should read this chapter to understand these hot topics, but apply your own skepticism, research, wisdom, and reasoning. The last topic on

Christian Nationalism is the most important to read as, in some ways, it encompasses all the others.

I sincerely hope you find this book useful. Please send me a note with feedback (good or bad) via:

Web: http://www.spiritualhumanist.info (use <u>Contact Us</u>)

Email: humanismforparents@spiritualhumanist.info

I - Overview of Humanism

Humanism is a broad philosophy or belief system that ranges from the strict Atheists to the agnostic/religious Unitarian Universalists. The roots of Humanism go back to Greek philosophy in the sixth century B.C.E. with Xenophanes who refused to recognize Gods who are actually involved in society[1]. The modern basis of Humanism, however, really stems from the Renaissance where intellectuals attempted to explain everything in terms of reason and logic and when the scientific method was established. At the time, humanists used the word *Umanista* to describe themselves as studiers of *humanitatis*, what we call liberal arts. The word *Humanism* was in fact not coined until 1808 in Germany[2]. In the middle of the 19th century, it began to take on its modern meaning when the Humanistic Religious Association formed in London, England.

One of the better modern definitions of Humanism is from Corliss Lamont, a popular author and proponent of Humanism:

> "Humanism, having its ultimate faith in humankind, believes that human beings possess the power or potentiality of solving their own problems, through reliance primarily upon reason and scientific method applied with courage and vision."[3]

Unfortunately, he included the phrase "ultimate faith in humankind". Faith is not what we are after as it implies belief without evidence or reasoning and some humanists still have faith in a God while living a Humanistic life. Other definitions stress the anti-religion or anti-faith aspect of Humanism even more. The definition from Wikipedia is also quite good:

> "Humanism is a broad category of ethical philosophies that affirm the dignity and worth of all people, based on the ability to determine right and wrong by appeal to universal human qualities—particularly rationalism."[4]

The key here is that we must base right versus wrong, our outlook on life, and how we decide to behave, on reason and intellect and not on faith or the possibility of a supernatural being.

At a very high level, the International Ethical and Humanist Union defined a set of modern Humanist principles. These include:

- Humanism is ethical. It affirms the worth, dignity and autonomy of the individual and the right of every human being.

- Humanism is rational. It seeks to use science creatively.

- Humanism supports democracy and human rights.

- Humanism insists that personal liberty must be combined with social responsibility.

- Humanism is a response to the widespread demand for an alternative to dogmatic religion.

- Humanism values artistic creativity and imagination.

- Humanism is a life stance aiming at the maximum possible fulfillment through the cultivation of ethical and creative living.

There have also been three Humanist Manifestos published to date. Free thinkers and Unitarian ministers published the first manifesto in 1933. The American Humanist Association published the most recent manifesto in 2002. The key statements in the Humanist Manifesto III are:

- Knowledge of the world is derived by observation, experimentation, and rational analysis.

- Humans are an integral part of nature, the result of unguided evolutionary change.

- Ethical values are derived from human need and interest as tested by experience.

- Life's fulfillment emerges from individual participation in the service of humane ideals.

- Humans are social by nature and find meaning in relationships.

- Working to benefit society maximizes individual happiness.

Frederick Edwords did a superb job of articulating the Humanist philosophy in his 1984 publication of *The Humanist Philosophy in Perspective*. He cleverly broke out basic (or core) principles from tentative beliefs about the world. He was attempting to address issues with previous manifestos and documents where they made claims about the world that are more personal and culturally specific and are not strictly core Humanist beliefs.

Humanism includes atheists, seculars, skeptics, agnostics, religious, non-theists, Brights*, and others who believe Humanity need to take responsibility for who we are and for our actions. If you take all of these groups into account there are reportedly 1.1 billion Humanists in the world (placing Humanism 3rd in ranking as a belief system), though only a small fraction would actually identify themselves as Humanists. One of the issues is that Humanism doesn't have a unifying belief as religions do and therefore Humanists don't naturally bond into a single group. Most Humanists just want to live their own moral, ethical lives without others telling them what to believe and without telling others what to believe. Therefore, what makes them Humanists is more of a lack of reliance on religion or a deity (whether or not they believe one exists) than proactive faith.

Nevertheless, recent world events have started to awaken this sleeping giant. The 9/11 attacks on the World Trade Center have re-shown us just how dangerous true faith can be. The attackers were just following the instructions in their holy book and truly believed they would go to heaven and be welcomed as heroes; really it is hard to blame them if they truly believe. This is just one of many examples where religion has been the cause of horrific events.

---

* Paul Geisert and Mynga Futrell coined the term Bright in 2003. They wanted a positive sounding term to describe people with a naturalistic worldview, without casting that worldview as a negative response to religion.

re has been a slow progression towards a

ere are people who now refer to America as a

a country that was founded on religious

to not believe in a Christian God. We

the concept of *separation of church and state* and it is in

impossible to elect someone to a high office in this country if they don't claim to be a Christian. Citizens in a Colorado town recently recalled their Mayor because he refused to say the pledge of allegiance because of the reference to God. Sam Harris, in his clever articulation, points out that statistically most intelligent people don't believe in God[*] and 100% of Congress[†] says they do believe in God, so most of them are either lying or are stupid.

There is a cultural and religious war beginning in the United States of America between theocratic leaders and proponents of freedom of religion and separation of church and state.

The thought of having modern weapons of mass destruction in the hands of medieval, intolerant, fundamental theocracies and having a cultural and religious war in America for the right to believe as we wish has pushed many otherwise quiet Humanists into becoming activists. On one side of this activism is *The New Atheism* as recently reported in *Wired*. They argue that faith in any form is dangerous and we have to rid the

---

[*] There have been 43 studies since 1927 and nearly all of them concur. Recent studies include those from Michael Shermer in *How We Believe*, and one due out shortly from R. Elisabeth Cornwell and Michael Stirrat that Richard Dawkins references in his book *The GOD Delusion*.

[†] That is, up until March of 2007 when Rep. Pete Stark (D-CA) publicly acknowledged he does not believe in a supreme being. The declaration makes him the highest-ranking elected official and first congressional representative to proclaim to be an atheist.

world of faith-based ideas and philosophies. The New Atheism is one extreme. Other faces of Humanist activism include:

- The popularity of relevant, secular books that ten years ago would not have been published.

- The surge of groups, forums, and blogs on Humanism, Atheism and other non-religious (or even anti-religious) topics.

- The creation of humanist churches.

- The establishment of Humanist Clergy like the Humanist Celebrant program, who can officiate at weddings, funerals, rites, etc.

- The popularity of Humanist and Atheist speakers.

Regardless of how radical any particular Humanist is, we all must conclude that we can no longer sit by and idly allow the unreasonable behavior of religions. The fact is, we cannot prove or disprove the existence of God; by the teachings of religion, we cannot question the books that define that religion, which is a circular argument[*]. Unproven religious beliefs have significant influence on governments, politics, and education. Many of these religions have shortsighted thinking because they believe that life on Earth is short-lived and will soon end[†].

------

[*] Circular arguments are those where the definition depends on the word or concept itself. To properly debate a point, the point cannot rely on itself.

[†] E.g., some don't think we need to worry about global warming because of the pending apocalypse.

Humanism for Parents

Whether or not there is a God or any particular religion is right, we have to define our ethics, morals, laws, and our standards for right and wrong on Human standards and we have to hold the Human race accountable for the health, both physical and spiritual, of our selves and our planet.

II - The Basis of Morality

One of the most frustrating topics of conversation between Humanists (especially those who don't believe in God) and religious people is morality. Many religious people have the mistaken understanding that their Holy Book, as the written word of God, defines our morality. There are many reasons why some ancient text isn't the basis for our morality. These include:

- Every society in recorded history has a moral code and many of them don't have a Bible or they have a completely different one than the Judeo/Christian Bible. If the book is the source of morality, how did all these other societies come up with morality?

- All societies have common attributes that they consider *good*: bravery, honesty, generosity, and compassion are examples. No book that is common to all these societies defines these to be *good*.

- Moral statements found in the bible predate the New Testament. "No original moral concepts of any significance can be found in the New Testament," says Victor Stenger[5]. Even common concepts like the Golden Rule are present in many societies, some prior to Jesus; in the 4th century B.C.E., Isocrates said, "Do not do to others what would anger you if done to you by others"[6].

- Some would argue that the Ten Commandments are the root of western codified law, but few of the Ten Commandments even apply to society in general. Depending on which version of the Commandments you use, only 6, 8, and 9 apply to our daily moral behavior[*].

- Scientists have seen moral and altruistic behavior in a number of animal species[7]. It is difficult to say a book defines morality when the species can't read.[†]

Modern evolutionary psychology is consistent and clear that morality and ethics have foundations in biology and evolution. Morality is common in societies because of the evolutionary advantages from *reciprocal altruism*[‡] and *kin selection*[§]. Robert Wright puts it well:

> "Sympathy, empathy, compassion, conscience, guilt, remorse, even the very sense of justice, the sense that doers of good deserve reward and doers of bad deserve punishment – all these can now be viewed as vestiges of organic history…"[8]

---

[*] These are: *You shall not murder, You shall not steal,* and *You shall not bear false witness.*

[†] Examples include that dogs often adopt orphaned cats, squirrels, ducks and even tigers; dolphins support sick or injured animals; male baboons cover the rear as the troop retreats.

[‡] Reciprocal Altruism is where two species not related by genes help each other to survive. The highest form of this is symbiosis where their lives are dependent on each other. Altruism helps both species survive and therefore propagate genes and it encourages altruism in general, as species that are willing to be reciprocally altruistic are more likely to survive.

[§] Kin Selection is where two species related by genes are more willing to sacrifice themselves in order to keep kin alive. This propagates like-genes and therefore increases the chances that those genes survive.

Parenting without Religion

Marc Hauser in *Moral Minds* has performed significant testing on moral attitudes. He believes there is a universal moral grammar that is driving our judgments and operates below the conscious level. He concluded this when he found a high correlation of moral responses across societies and religions and even across religious and non-religious people.

It is true however, that morality is much easier and cleaner when defined by a God or religion. If God doesn't define our morality, then community and culture define it and it is then up for debate. Morality, what is considered right versus wrong, changes over time (slavery being one of the best examples). This lack of a clear, timeless definition of right and wrong is one of the main issues many people have today with any secular belief.

The answer lies in what Sam Harris suggests, "A rational approach to ethics becomes possible once we realize that questions of right and wrong are really questions about the happiness and suffering of sentient creatures"[9]. We as Humanists have to look at the physical, mental, and spiritual happiness of other humans and gauge righteousness on that.

There are reasoned scientific arguments for a basis for morality separate from religion. However, these are mostly academic or among the intelligentsia. When it comes down to day-to-day living, we need to have codified law that defines what is right and wrong. The law must be flexible enough to deal with changing times and mores and stringent enough to be clear to the populous and supportable by the courts.

Humanism for Parents

From a parental standpoint, you must merge your own morality with the laws of the state and combine that with an empathy and compassion for others — a sense of instilling happiness and avoiding suffering. The trick is to do this for the long term. It does no good to give your children constant happiness through electronics and candy and not prepare them for the world. For a person to be happy throughout life, he or she has to have self-respect, confidence, and a spiritually fulfilling life. Teaching a child these can be a difficult process, but one that is required for a happy, fulfilled life.

The key is to teach your child to consider the happiness of others. When a child comes to us to tattle, we always ask if he or she is trying to help the one they are tattling on or hurt him or her. If the answer isn't to help (which usually manifests as hesitation or no answer), then we tell him or her to go away. The point we are making is that they should be coming to us when they are trying to help someone, not to hurt them.

III - Tenets of Good Parenting

This section is common to all types of families, regardless of religion or belief. It isn't strictly the intent of this book, but the book would not be complete without it. The information here is Humanistic only in that it uses research, reason, and observation and not the Bible or faith. The Bible has some *interesting* parenting techniques that are abhorrent to us today[*].

Parenting today is very different than it was 50 years ago. Beyond the changes with divorce rate, same-sex marriages, and birth control, there have been significant cultural changes. My father grew up during the depression and started supporting his family at the age of 12 when his father disappeared. His idea of an ideal father was one that provided for the family consistently and who didn't beat his wife or children. He succeeded tremendously and I give him a great deal of credit and respect for breaking that cycle of child abuse. Nevertheless, today we would consider him a neglectful if not outright abusive parent because of his lack of emotional support and his willingness to use a belt for punishment. Times have clearly changed.

This topic isn't just for traditional parents. Anyone who has influence on a child has a parenting role. This includes grandparents and other members of the extended family, friends and neighbors,

---

[*] These include harsh corporal punishment, stoning, and murder (e.g. "Anyone who curses his father or mother shall be put to death" Leviticus 20:9)

schoolteachers, family aides, community workers, and even doctors and nurses.

We happen to have four great children; mature, happy, confident, and capable. People frequently ask me how we do this. Generally, I answer with something like the following:

> "There are generally only two things that drive children. They happen to contradict each other, which is what makes parenting so interesting. The first is that they want to understand the world around them and their way of doing that is by pushing all the limits to see what works and what doesn't. The second is that they want, above anything else, the attention (good or bad) of their parents. So, if you don't clearly show them where the limits are, then they will keep pushing past them and if you don't give them attention when they are good, they will do whatever they need to do to get some (any) attention."[10]

To us, these two aspects of children explain almost all of their behavior and represent the basis of how we parent. At a very base level, good parenting consists of the following three requirements:

Unconditional Love and Care

Love in this case is the broad meaning of it – not necessarily the love between two partners or even parent/child love. Every child needs to feel he or she has consistent, unconditional love. This teaches the child the value of loving, caring relationships and aids in their ability to develop meaningful, long-term relationships when they are older. Early psychological studies of orphaned children where scientists provided only emotionless care resulted in both emotional maturity issues and stunted physical development.*

Consistent Limit Setting

This is the setting of reasonable boundaries and then consistently enforcing those settings. Boundaries are set to teach the child what behavior is unacceptable. If you are inconsistent, the child learns that boundaries can be pushed and it isn't clear what is and isn't acceptable behavior. In addition, if the boundaries are unreasonable or if punishment is inconsistent or too punitive then the child will eventually rebel. The article in *Archives of Disease in Childhood* tells us, "Many habitual delinquents have been the subject of an indulgent lack of discipline interspersed with unpredictable and sudden outbursts of harsh discipline."[11]

This doesn't mean you can't be spontaneous occasionally. If the child has done something particularly good or you feel like bending your rules for a special occasion, feel free. However, this has to be under your control. If you let the child bend the rules or force you to bend, then you are being inconsistent and the child no longer knows what the boundaries really are.

---

* Unfortunately, this comes from my memory of a study I looked at in psychology class in college and I can't find the reference.

Development

This is an attempt to help the child obtain his or her full potential. This includes physical, mental, and spiritual aspects. Generally, this means providing diverse input and experiences in early life followed by support and encouragement in the teenage years. Of course, it also includes a healthy diet that meets the nutritional needs of a growing body.

Being a Good Parent

There really isn't one right way to parent and children vary greatly. The American Academy of Family Physicians suggests the following guidelines to help your children grow up healthy and happy[12]:

- Show your love. Every day, tell your children: 'I love you. You're special to me.' Give lots of hugs and kisses.

- Listen when your children talk. Listening to your children tells them that you think they're important and that you're interested in what they have to say.

- Make your children feel safe. Comfort them when they're scared. Show them you've taken steps to protect them.

- Provide order in their lives. Keep a regular schedule of meals, naps and bedtimes. If you have to change the schedule, tell them about the changes ahead of time.

- Praise your children. When your children learn something new or behave well, tell them you're proud of them.

- Criticize the behavior, not the child. When your child makes a mistake, don't say, 'You were bad.' Instead, explain what the child did wrong. For example, say: 'Running into the street without looking isn't safe.' Then tell the child what to do instead: 'First, look both ways for cars.'

- Be consistent. Your rules don't have to be the same ones other parents have, but they do need to be clear and consistent. If two parents are raising a child, both need to use the same rules. Also, make sure baby sitters and relatives know, and follow, your family rules.

- Spend time with your children. Do things together, like reading, walking, playing and cleaning house. What children want most is your attention.

Of course, these are just guidelines. Every child is different and you have to be cognizant of variations. For example, low blood sugar or being tired can cause temporary bad behavior. A small child who has not had a nap can get quite irritable.

Dealing with Relatives

Related to being consistent with your child is how you deal with being a Humanist, or Atheist, in a religious family setting. When visiting grandparents, uncles and aunts, or even cousins, you need to be aware of their beliefs. And more importantly, how compelled they are to preach their religion to others. Many religious family members, especially grandparents, feel it is their duty to teach your children their religion. They may even feel it is their responsibility to *save* the child.

There are various ways of how to deal with this. The one you use depends on how adamant (pushy) your relatives are and how strongly you feel about your beliefs.

- As the saying goes, *when in Rome, live as Romans.* You can just ignore the situation and let the family members do their religious acts. This needs to include some discussion with your children about the differences in belief. You may also need to discuss how it is okay to keep silent sometimes when you disagree with someone.

- Attempt to get the family members to stay silent on the subject. This is a more difficult discussion, but with the family members and not your children. If the family members are flexible, this may be your best choice, as it doesn't confuse the children.

- Spend less time with the family members. This is a harsh answer, but sometimes the only one if you are significantly opposed to each other and can't come to some resolution or civil standoff.

Another consideration is who to choose as *guardians* for your children (who do you indicate your children will go to in your will if you die). This is frequently a very difficult question and depends a great deal on many factors. Their religious stance is one such factor, as are their parenting ability, their financial situation, and how much they will respect your wishes. There is no definitive answer I can give you here; just consider all of the factors carefully.

IV - Humanist Parenting & Spirituality

As you can see from *Tenants of Good Parenting*, parenting in a Humanist household is much like parenting in a strictly religious household. The primary difference then is that there are some aspects of a holistically healthy family that religions naturally provide that are more difficult without religion. These practices center around what I call *spirituality*. The word itself is debatable, but in this context, I'm referring to aspects of spirituality that have to do with the mental health and happiness of the individual and the family. There are rituals, traditions, and practices, commonly found within the religious sphere, that provide spirituality and that are frequently missing in the lives of non-religious individuals and families.

Spirituality is a key element of a person being *healthy* in the holistic way. Overall health is not just about the physical aspects of not being sick or being able to climb twenty flights of stairs. To be fully healthy (and happy) one has to have balance in various aspects of their life. These aspects include physical, mental, and spiritual areas. Despite what some might say, spirituality is not in conflict with Humanism or even Atheism. Sam Harris put it nicely: "While there is surely an opposition between reason and faith ... there is none between reason and love or reason and spirituality"[13].

Religion has natural (comfortable) ways to participate in safe social interaction, to practice rituals that help bind people together, and traditions that show us our place in the progression of time and our relationship to the past. These elements do not naturally occur in a Humanist household. In particular, the following are areas that a Humanist must pay special attention to since they are not naturally present:

- Periodic social gatherings with like-minded families

- A connection with the past

- Various Rituals that help a person naturally flow through life

- Community Traditions (group/social traditions beyond the family)

- Music and Singing

- Periodic sessions of some form of meditation

Spirituality is clearly possible without religion, but we don't have thousands of years of practice, tradition, and ritual to accomplish it so naturally. Instead, we have to work at it by proactively providing various aspects of spirituality that religions naturally provide.

Traditions & Rituals

Historically, rituals are abundant: from minor practices like shaking hands, bowing, or saluting to complex practices around marriage and even barbaric ones like ritual sacrifices. Rituals are present in every known society in history[14].

We have many minor rituals we do today that evolved over time in society; however, these are not important for this discussion. Specifically of interest here are those rituals that religion has historically prescribed and which are primarily (but not exclusively) practiced in a religious setting today. In particular, this means the various rituals around life-events, like:

- Birth Celebrations

- Commitment and Marriage Celebrations

- Separation or Divorce Rituals

- Memorials and Funerals

- Other less traditional rituals

For many of these rituals, you can ask a close friend or relative to perform the ceremony, though check on state rules, especially around marriage.

Birth Celebrations

Birth celebrations are present in every society in the world. They vary greatly from baptisms in the west to the bonding celebration in Bali when the community recognizes a child is alive at 6 months of age and the child's feet touch the ground for the first time. Most of these celebrations have a religious context and some include the tradition of circumcision, which is unneeded as there is no medical basis for performing the surgery[*].

In the modern, non-religious home, celebrations of birth frequently involve an email or some phone calls with everyone being

---

[*] Some recent studies seem to indicate male circumcision may lower the risk of contracting AIDS in men.

happy and saying *congratulations* or maybe sending an announcement card. What they don't generally include is a more formal acceptance into the world by close family members and friends or the concept of a guardian outside of the parents (e.g. a godparent).

We need a more formal celebration of life that includes some inspiring words and some ritual. You can find a Humanist Celebrant (or officiate), or the other possibility is having the new guardians preside over the celebration. In any case, you should have some form of guardian assigned to the child and talk with them beforehand about your expectations around accepting the responsibility. Too often nowadays people are assigned to be guardians and don't know what it means, so they don't really take on the responsibilities. Ideally, you would also form a will and indicate these guardians are to become the legal guardians of your children if you die.

Commitment or Marriage Celebrations

In many states today, laws have made it possible for couples to marry themselves or to have almost anyone preside over the marriage, though you should always check your state's laws. This can be as simple as committing to each other and behaving as if you are married or as complex as a full-blown traditional wedding with a non-religious minister.

Wedding traditions vary over the world and between races and cultures. The specifics of the wedding are completely up to the individuals and should reflect their beliefs and philosophies. The American Atheists have a nice article on some wedding ceremony options for Humanists[15]. Local chapters of Humanists, Atheists, or Brights can also refer you to qualified people to preside over the ceremony.

Separation or Divorce Rituals

Many religious organizations are today recognizing divorce and the importance of providing a ritual around it to help the participants move on. Both *Beliefnet* (Christian) and *Ritual Well* (Jewish) have pages on rituals around separation and divorce.

The same options for marriage ceremonies are available for divorce or separation. More important to consider here are the children that are involved. In the case of children, separation and divorce are immensely complex and you must carefully consider the ramifications. Even the decision of whether or not to separate or divorce can tear a person apart. If you choose to separate or divorce, I strongly suggest you obtain counseling for both yourself and your children from a reputable, experienced family counselor.

Memorials and Funerals

I have had the unfortunate privilege to be a part of many memorials and funerals through my life; from two of my brothers' funerals (when I was 12 and 14) to friends and other family including my parents. The best of these have invariably been the ones that celebrated the person's life rather than concentrating on their death. Nowadays you can create a multimedia presentation (or even just a slide show) of pictures and events that represent the person, provide drinks and music, and toast the life of the individual. This has a lot more meaning than many of the traditional religious funerals and is much more uplifting.

The most important thing is to provide the understanding, and therefore the healing, that the family and friends need. Generally, this needs to fall within the confines of what the deceased person would have wanted done. When my father passed away, he specifically asked that we not get up in front of everyone and talk about all the great things he had done. In his mind, his life should speak for itself and people either knew him for what he did or they didn't know him, and in either case, they didn't need to be told. We honored this and when I spoke to everyone, I instead read a poem that my siblings and I felt represented my father.

The good news for non-religious people is that there are no real legal aspects of a funeral, so any reasonable ceremony can be performed by anyone; no qualifications are specifically required. Therefore, finding a Humanist Celebrant or a friend to talk is perfectly acceptable and in many cases, a family member is the most appropriate.

Other Less Traditional Rituals

You can consider many less traditional, but still practiced, rituals. These usually recognize a person's progression through life and provide a sense of belonging to a community, as we all experience some of these. They include rituals like the following:

- Hand Fasting (an old Celtic tradition of binding before marriage)

- Adulthood

- High School or College Graduation

- First House

- New Job

- Anniversary

- Conversion (hopefully to becoming a Humanist)

- Adoption

- Menstruation or Menopause

- Coming out (announcement of being homosexual)

- Debutante Announcement

Holidays

Many people around the world perceive certain holidays to be religious, and more specifically, Christian. However, they have a much more convoluted history than that and are clearly not simply Christian holidays. Many of them have roots in pre-Christian civilization.

Atheists and even some Humanists try to abandon many of the supposed Christian holidays or try to establish similar ones that can replace the common ones. This is difficult at best and is often uncomfortable for family and friends as the society in general celebrate these holidays. There is no need to be this radical as these holidays aren't specifically Christian.

Christmas

In 1984, the Supreme Court, in *Lynch v. Donnelly*, ruled that public displays of Christmas were permissible, because "The display is sponsored by the city to celebrate the Holiday and to depict the origins of that Holiday,". The majority wrote, "These are legitimate secular purposes."[16]

The following is a quote about the origins of Christmas in The Buffalo News:

"The earliest reference to Christmas being marked on Dec. 25 comes from the second century after Jesus' birth. It is considered likely the first Christmas celebrations were in reaction to the Roman Saturnalia, a harvest festival that marked the winter solstice - the return of the sun - and honored Saturn, the god of sowing. Saturnalia was a rowdy time, much opposed by the more austere leaders among the still-minority Christian sect. Christmas developed, one scholar says, as a means of replacing worship of the sun with worship of the Son. By 529 A.D., after Christianity had become the official state religion of the Roman Empire, Emperor Justinian made Christmas a civic holiday. The celebration of Christmas reached its peak - some would say its worst moments - in the medieval period when it became a time for conspicuous consumption and unequaled revelry."[17]

The actual Roman holiday was a three-day event starting on December 22nd (the winter solstice) and lasting three days. It was said that the sun died on the 22nd and rose again three days later (sound familiar?) on the 25th, which was the climax of the celebration.

The story of Santa Claus is even more convoluted. By some world encyclopedias, *Santa* was a common name for Nimrod throughout Asia Minor. This was also the same fire god who came down the chimneys of the ancient Pagans and who inspired infant sacrifices. Today Santa Claus comes from *Saint Nicholas*. Washington Irving, in 1809, is responsible for remaking the original old, stern bishop of this same name into the new *jolly St. Nick*. Most of the rest of America's Christmas traditions are even more recent than this.

Easter

Easter also has its roots in non-Christian tradition. The name comes to us, not from the Bible, but from Eastre, the Teutonic goddess of Spring[18]. It is associated with the Spring Equinox and is a time of fertility. The traditions come to us from the Babylonians - Christian priests visited them from Rome in the 6th century and brought back the ritual; they adapted it to help celebrate the death and resurrection of Christ, but many of the Pagan traditions, like egg painting, remained*.

---

* See http://www.christiananswers.net/q-eden/edn-t020.html or http://en.wikipedia.org/wiki/Easter

Easter is also associated with Passover. It is difficult to tell from historical records, but many believe Passover originated from the same Babylonian fertility rituals.

Connecting with the past

The Bible and many other documents give the religious a rich history with which to both teach and connect. With Humanism, it is more difficult as we don't really want to teach the stories out of the Bible (or other dogmatically followed books) and yet we need to have that connection to the past. Sam Harris put it well:

> "As a collection of self-regulating and continually dividing cells, you are also continuous with your genetic precursors: your parents, their parents and backward through tens of millions of generations -- at which point your ancestors begin looking less like men and women with bad teeth and more like pond scum."[19]

He has a wonderful writing style, but the point is that *we are all connected*, both with each other and with our past. I once read that if you go back 800 years then everyone in your geographical area are related and if you go back 1600 years, then everyone in the world is related. So if you take any one person in the distant past and know (or assume) they had enough children to survive and continue the process, then you are related to him or her.

There are a number of possible ways to connect with the past:

- Dive into your own genealogy. I did this and now have a book of about 120 pages detailing the history of our family, some of it going back to the 400 C.E. timeframe. We also have a wall of pictures in our living room of ancestors back to the 1800's. Seeing this so evident all the time helps the family to see the connection to the past and to appreciate who they are and how they came to be here.

- Make sure you keep in contact with your oldest living relatives. Frequently in America, we don't spend enough time with the eldest members of our family and so aren't seeing the connection to past people and past times.

- Read mythological books and other fun stories of the past. These stories usually teach something and help to connect us to a colorful past. Just read them as stories and not factual books.

- The same goes for the Bible and other *Books of God*. Don't be so worried about reading or telling the stories, just treat them with the same reason and skepticism you would treat any other book. They do have great things to say in many cases.

Life's passage

Generally, people like consistency and repetition in the form of traditions and rites. It is also important for people to feel a progression through life; this is especially relevant to young people who measure their self worth on the view of others and on how they relate to grown-ups (people who have already *made it*).

Some of the more day-to-day rituals are common enough for everyone (religious or not) and so we don't need to differentiate here. Rites of Passage are another matter; these are prevalent in religious families and generally completely absent in non-religious families. Even in many modern religious homes these rites that mark the passage of time, and tell a person they are progressing, aren't clear. Take as an example this true story:

> "When my father passed away, I remember wondering if I was now a man; and then immediately thought what an odd thought that was. How is it that a 45 year-old man with children and a successful career could not consider himself a 'man'? It took some thinking, but the answer was in the fact that there was never any point in my life where I recognized myself as being an adult/man. It was high school, then college, then starting a job, then getting married, having kids and building my career - nowhere did I reach a point where someone told me I *made it*"[20].

This story, though striking, probably isn't that unusual. You may laugh at someone not thinking they are a man at that age, but you would just be playing on the literal meaning of the word - it might be clear logically, but not emotionally. What is important here is that this person's upbringing didn't have the rites of passage that would have made it clear when he passed into adulthood.

The following sections take us through some phases/ages that are important to recognize. This includes some formality to make it clear the individual has passed on to the next phase of their life. Of course, these may not work well for you and you should consider how you would want to accomplish this in a way that makes sense for you.

Celebrating Reason

There are varying opinions on when children begin to recognize themselves as separate from the world. Each child is different so there is no exact age that this happens. However, sometime around the age of seven, a child starts to gain reason or self-awareness (some would say sentience). At that point, they recognize that actions have a result and that they can affect the world around them. In some countries (Japan for instance), society does not hold children accountable until they reach this age and then they hold children very accountable. In some religions, this is the first point that the child can understand enough of the religion to be able to participate in particular sacraments (e.g. First Communion in Catholicism).

We did not make this an elaborate celebration for our family or require anything specific of the child. However, we did have a *Seventh Celebration* for each child to recognize the passing into the *Age of Reason*. After this, we also started to make a point of including the child in decisions (or at least allowing him or her to offer opinions) and in getting them to begin to be responsible and accountable to the family as a team member (e.g. weekly chores).

Parenting without Religion

The *Seventh Celebration* in our household usually involved Mom and Dad spending a day with the child away from the other children in something fun (e.g. an amusement park) and having the entire family congratulate the child.

Recognizing Maturity

This may be the most important of all of these, the most difficult, and the one we have spent the most time on. In many religions, there is a rite of passage around the 13-year-old point. In Judaism, this is *Bar Mitzvah* or *Bat Mitzvah* that commemorates the beginning of adulthood. The important point here is that the religious practices are recognizing that the individual is now old enough to make decisions and be held accountable.

We need something just as important to the individual's life in a non-religious setting, but this one goes further than just this. We believe that it is a parent's job to prepare each child for the world and prepare him or her to be able to function reasonably well in it without the parent's presence. There needs to be specific recognition of this age. Because of that, and because of the social aspects of modern society, 13 years of age is probably too young. We celebrate this rite around 15 or 16 years of age.

Finally, there needs to be a clear demarcation point for the parents. This recognition of maturity is as much for the parents to begin to let go and not micro-manage as much as it is for the teenager to be recognized.

We have designed a complete program around this transition. We call it *Aostach* (a Gaelic word that roughly means the transition to maturity) that includes many topics and abilities that we think the individual should know or have before we recognize them for being mature, capable, and ready. These include various topics split into the following categories:

- Domestic Skills

- Financial Skills

- Safety and Survival

- Physical Fitness

- Daily Practical Knowledge

- Ethics, Morals, and Social Responsibilities

- Other

The culmination of this program is a stress test and a ceremony that shows everyone he or she has *graduated*. More importantly, the stance and attitude other adults in the household have toward this individual changes. Once passing this program, we consider the person a peer in the house generally with all the rights of another adult staying with us. Of course, there are caveats to this in case the teenager isn't a reasonable adult. We laid down basic expectations that we would have of an adult staying with us and held the individual accountable to these and to adult behavior.

This process helped our oldest child become a mature person with the self-respect and knowledge of someone who is ready for the world. It may not work for everyone and we are sure the specifics will change for everyone who tries this, but it is a successful method of having a rite of passage into *maturity* for a non-religious household.

Recognizing Adulthood

This is a more difficult topic as there isn't a clear point that a person becomes an adult. Additionally, in modern society, people are maturing into adulthood at a later and later point. The number of people still living at home* and unmarried at the age of 30 has increased dramatically[21]

For any particular individual, maturity into *adulthood* (this being based on a level of maturity rather than biological age) can vary greatly. However, generally in America, it is somewhere in their 20's. Religious families today don't commonly recognize this rite – they may have a rite of passage and refer to it as being an adult, but few today would call a 13-year-old an adult.

For our purposes, we want to celebrate the *coming of age* into adulthood as recognition of the maturity, ability and readiness of the individual, but even more importantly, it is recognition of their responsibility. You could look at it as almost a handoff of the reins and so it may be best to tie it to getting married or having a child.

---

* Many of the articles attribute this to the financial situation and inability to afford to live independently.

We wait until one of the following occurs:

- The individual gets engaged to be married.

- The individual announces that she (or the partner of he) is pregnant or is going to adopt a child.

- The individual is approaching his/her 30th birthday.

We have a large package of *stuff* to turn over at this point along with a conversation about the responsibilities of caring for others. The package includes the following:

- A complete set of pictures on DVDs (we have scanned in all in the past and take all new ones with a digital camera).

- An updated Genealogy Book about our family.

- Our yearly letters (my wife and I both write a letter to the kids once a year, her to each individually, myself to the group).

- A novella I wrote called *Reflections in the Dark* that contains what words of wisdom I can offer.

- Memorabilia from growing up (keepsakes, photo albums, etc.).

- Christmas (or winter solstice if you prefer) ornaments (we bought a new one each year for each child).

The point of this exercise and conversation is to make the individual aware that he or she is now independent and ready for the world and has the responsibilities of a full-fledged adult, especially now that he or she is becoming responsible for others (or at least of that age).

Social Interaction

Social gatherings are a critical part of social development for children and for happiness and connectivity with the community for adults. In a religious environment, these happen periodically (usually weekly) in the form of worship and Sunday school, or equivalent, and less often in socials that bring the religious community together.

Humanists can attend many of these events, but it won't be with a consistent group as it would be with a religious organization. The significant thing here is to be proactive about having and attending social events with like-minded people for both yourself and your children.

Some possible solutions include:

- Humanist Organizations (Brights, Atheists, Freethinkers, Skeptics, Unitarians, etc.) - find one in your area and join the organization. It isn't critical that you believe everything they espouse or that you like every person (do religious people like every person in their church?). What is critical is that you interact with like-minded people and that you provide this opportunity to your children.

- Online Forums and Groups - these are less useful in terms of social interaction, but they do provide a means of interacting with like-minded people, even if it isn't in person.

- Mother/Family Groups - These tend to be local groups for stay-at-home parents, finding one of these can be a great opportunity for repeatable social interaction with like-minded people.

- High Intelligence Organizations - most intelligent people are generally non-religious (only 7% of surveyed scientists believe in God[22]) and so you are likely to find Humanists there.[*]

Other Practices

There are additional practices that are even more difficult to handle. These have traditionally been prevalent in most religions and provide benefits to the congregation, but are not normally prevalent at all outside of religion.

Meditation

Meditation is common in religious gatherings through either prayer, or in some religions, chanting. Prayer is ultimately a form of meditation, especially repetitious prayers like the Catholic rosary. Science has shown that this kind of meditation has medicinal value through allowing the brain to enter an *Alpha State* that aids the body's natural healing processes[23]. Statistically, those who pray tend to be healthier than those who don't.

---

[*] You can get a partial list on our site at http://spiritualhumanist.info/hi-iq-groups.shtml or Yahoo! maintains a list.

Humanists can easily take on the Eastern civilization practice of meditation. However, this infrequently happens. The benefits are not obvious at first and it takes time away from busy schedules. Other options include silent thinking and saying thanks before meals, or simply attempting to have your children (and you) sit quietly with their eyes closed for a few minutes periodically.

Group Singing

Group singing is an uplifting and binding experience for groups. Most religions offer some form of hymns or songs that congregations sing in a group. Singing in a group setting is an important aspect of social interaction and group spirituality. This is natural in a religious setting with gospel singing, but quite unnatural (except for those select few who are good at it) in a non-religious setting.

I suggest having music playing in the house at times that everyone enjoys and try to encourage family members to sing-along. Another option is to go to concerts periodically with the family, especially ones who have the audience sing-along. Finally, you can join a Universal Unitarian church. These non-denominational churches offer a very open service that frequently includes singing. Many Humanists attend UU churches periodically.

An Open Mind

Depending on your culture, background, and beliefs, there may be other practices that you need to think about or adjust. Keep your mind open and be alert for opportunities to provide a spiritual, fulfilling life for your children. Don't relegate religion to the completely useless; instead try to learn from the thousands of years of religious history and the many positive things religions teach us. Use common sense and rational thought to apply what you learn from religion to your life and to the upbringing of your children.

V - Religious Conflict

There is a religion-based cultural war going on in America today. It has been brewing for many years, but is heating up in this first decade of the new century. Since America began, people who did not really believe in a particular religion or God were allowed to believe as they wished. That is exactly how they wanted it and they were happy to leave others alone as well. This *Timothy Leary* style of philosophy is one of the primary reasons there hasn't been a united Humanist movement. We haven't had a single unifying belief or force to drive us; instead, we just didn't believe in the unifying beliefs others had.

However, two things at the start of this century have changed that. First were the 9/11 attacks on the World Trade Center. These were religion-based attacks and show just how dangerous religion can be. We all knew of the many religion-based atrocities of the past. A short list might include:

- Attempted genocide of followers of another faith (e.g. the Jewish Holocaust, ethnic cleansing in former Yugoslavia, etc.)

- Suicide bombers taught to believe that martyrs go straight to Paradise.

- Slavery supported by scripture.

- Atrocities against women (e.g. female circumcision).

- Holy wars - killing others in the name of their gods.

- Witch trials in Europe and America.

- The Crusades.

- The Inquisition.

- Persecution of Heretics (e.g. Galileo for suggesting that the Earth orbits the Sun).

- Mass suicides of cult-members following a charismatic leader.

Nevertheless, in America, we all tend to think of those events as in the past or somewhere else. That ignorant belief went away with the 9/11 attacks.

The 9/11 attacks were committed by true believers of Islam who are told, via the Koran, that if they die as martyrs they will go to heaven and get 72 beautiful virgins (as well as 28 young boys)[24]. Because of the prevalence of their religion back on Earth, their communities honor their surviving families with gifts and respect, for they were true believers and followed their holy book to the best of their ability. These attacks make it abundantly clear that we can no longer tolerate this kind of religious fundamentalism.

The other change has been brewing for many years. That is the fact that the religious right has entered politics and is trying to turn the country into a modern form of a theocracy. Many organizations are arguing that this is a Christian Nation and that our founding fathers founded it to be a Christian Nation[25] (apparently, we all misunderstood the freedom of religion section of the Constitution).

These frightening changes should be keeping all of us up at night. However, there is good news as well. These changes have brought many

Parenting without Religion

Humanists out of the closet and made them become more active. There are groups springing up all over to support separation of church and state, religious freedom, and a democratic way of life. Publishers have also joined the conflict with mainstream publishers supplying relevant books for both sides of the argument.

These changes point to a looming conflict between religious fundamentalists and free thinkers. This conflict had its infancy in the Renaissance where science became a disciplined practice with tangible results that countered established religious dogma. A couple of notable events ensued along the way were when the Church tried Galileo for saying that the Earth revolved around the Sun, and when Darwin published his groundbreaking books on Evolution. This conflict is one that needs to happen! Unfortunately, there is no telling who will win. Will we become a theocracy and fall back into medieval religious dogmatism and control, or will we break free from the constraints of religion? It is up to you and I.

From a parenting standpoint, this is going to play out as conflicts on the school grounds. Religious children today are becoming more vocal and adamant because their parents are talking about the conflict and their beliefs more. Many non-religious children are more willing to say they are Atheist or Humanist than they were in the past because we are also talking about the conflict and our beliefs more.

This may make for some difficult conversations for your children. The most important thing you can do is make sure your children are informed. Rely on knowledge and reason to hold the day. Encourage them to speak their mind, but to think it through first and to do it with patience and reasoning. Children and the school ground is where the fight is the most vital. If our children can collectively decide that we need to use reason and intellect, and not faith, to figure out how we should behave, then by the time the next generation is in charge, we will secure a country where we are free to believe as we wish, even if that means not believing.

The following chapters may help them in their quest for understanding.

VI - Humanism for Kids

This section is for children up to and including the *Age of Reason* (roughly 7 to 9 years of age). Every child matures differently and may need the explanations in this section at different ages. You can use these explanations as they are, let the child read the section on his or her own or take it and modify it to match your situation and beliefs. I have laid out this section as a series of questions and answers that you can read individually or as a group. I've also intentionally kept the answers simple, as I've found that children of this age don't really need in-depth answers. If you are finding your child is not satisfied with these answers, try the section on *Humanism for Teens*. Finally, I've tried to order the questions logically so that the next question flows from the previous answer whenever possible.

~~~~~~~~~~~~~~~~

Is there a God?

The meaning of God is very different to different people. For some it is just another name for *nature* or *life* and for others it means a being that is very powerful and looks over us and cares about us. We can't tell for sure whether this type of God exists. Many people in the world believe that it does, but they don't know for sure – they rely on faith.

What is Faith?

Faith is the belief in something without any evidence. So, there isn't proof, but they feel so strongly that they believe anyway. You can't argue with a person who believes by faith because he or she isn't using logic or reason.

How did people start believing in God?

The world is full of very strange things that are hard to explain without modern science. Hurricanes, volcanoes, earthquakes, and solar eclipses are some of the examples. People believed someone must be causing them and so they named them Gods.

The other reason is that life was very hard, many people suffered, and many died. It was easier to believe that the person dying went somewhere nice when they died.

Where do we go when we die?

Our bodies go away through either burial or cremation and are used in the continuing creation and death that is the cycle of life. We also live on in the memories of others.

What is the Bible (or other holy book)?

These books are very special to the people who believe in them. In fact, some people believe that God wrote their Holy Book (through men). But, those books are not historical books – they are stories meant to teach people how to live. In the case of the Christian Bible for example, there is no historical information that Jesus ever existed, but the Bible tells many useful stories about Jesus.

Who created us?

Humans were created through a process called evolution. Evolution is where life changes over a very long time to be able to survive better. These changes create new types of life and over a very, very long time, Humans arose.

How do we know how to behave?

Most people learn how to behave from their parents, teachers, and friends. People that behave well are rewarded with respect and friendship and people who behave badly are punished. There is also a good general rule called *The Golden Rule*. This rule says that you should treat others the same way you want to be treated. So, if you are trying to decide if you should do something you need to ask yourself if that is how you would want others to behave toward you.

What are we if we are not religious?

We are called Humanists because we believe in the Human race: that each of us must take responsibility for ourself and that we all have to take responsibility for Humanity and Earth. We believe in using reason and our brains to solve problems, and that we don't need to rely on faith or a God to make things better.

There are many other names that someone might call us including: Atheist, Heathen, Heretic, Pagan, and Godless. Some of these are mean names and don't really apply to us and others might apply, but some people don't like those names and think they are bad. Humanist is a name that we can all accept and that people can recognize as being good for the Human race.

What else do Humanists believe?

We believe that we get knowledge of the way the world works through the scientific method, which includes watching things, guessing how it works, experimenting, and trying to understand.

We believe Humans are one part of nature and are the result of evolutionary changes over a very long time.

We believe that our understanding of right and wrong comes from human need and interest and that it changes with experience and knowledge.

We believe that our happiness comes from being good and doing service to other Humans.

We believe that Humans like being with other Humans and that we find happiness and meaning making and being with friends.

What is the Scientific Method?

The scientific method is what we use to try to make sure we have the truth. It uses the following process:

1.   Watch things.

2.   Come up with an idea that might explain what you saw.

3.   Make some guesses based on your idea.

4.   Test your guesses.

5.   Start over (and include the test results).

We also share our theories and ideas with others and we consider all ideas. When we are this open and we talk this much, new and interesting theories and predictions come out. These get us closer and closer to the truth.

Is science ever wrong?

Yes, scientists can be wrong, but they are doing the best they can given the things we know today. Each theory gets better and better at explaining what we see and so is closer and closer to the truth. One of the most important things about science is that it is always open to re-thinking; this allows us to improve our knowledge all the time. Sometimes even our mistakes can give us new and wonderful things (like new medicines for example.) We are continually questioning how things work and this helps us understand them better.

Should I tell people we are Humanists?

Yes, of course. We are proud of being Humanist and we think it is a good way to live. Your friends may be surprised if you tell them that you don't believe in God, but that is because they were brought up in a family that has faith and does not question religion. Just explain to them that people believe many different things, some believe in their God, some in other Gods and many people don't believe in God at all, or at least think that we have to live good lives independent of religion.

But, you don't need to be mean about it or tell people they are stupid for believing in a God. Let them believe the way they want or the way their parents do and we will believe the way we do.

What about Christmas, isn't that a religious holiday?

Actually, Christmas started as a celebration of the middle of winter and the turning towards spring. That is why it is celebrated December 25th. It sounds like a Christian holiday because we use the Christian name for it. Many non-Christian people celebrate Christmas.

What do I do when Grandma and Grandpa start acting religious?

Different people believe different ways. You will come across others who believe and practice religion. It is best to let them practice religion and to be polite. You don't need to object, but you also don't have to practice as they do.

VII - Humanism for Teens

This section is very similar to the *Humanism for Kids* section, but the intended audience is teenagers that tend to want a deeper and more complete explanation. Teenagers are not as willing to accept a simple statement as an answer. Much of the information here may be redundant with the rest of this book, but it is in a question & answer format and is valuable to have in one location that you can have your teenager read.

~~~~~~~~~~~~~~~~

Is there a God?

This depends on how one defines *God*. Some definitions are so general that they would include nature. Einstein, for instance, referred to God a number of times. However, he didn't mean a God like the Christian God, but rather nature and the glorious universe. However, many people have a very specific meaning of God with the most common being the God of Abraham (the Christian, Jewish, and Islamic God). We can't prove or disprove the existence of this kind of God. In this case, our understanding of God is from sacred books (like the Bible). These books both claim to be the word of God and say that we can't doubt the book. The fact that the book is the only thing that says you can't doubt the book is circular – it is like me writing a book that says Yoda is a God and that Yoda told me that, so it has to be true.

Where do we go when we die?

Many religious people believe that good people go to heaven, which is a wonderful place that rewards them, and that bad people go to hell, which punishes them terribly for whatever they did wrong in life. One problem with this is that each religion and, in fact, each faction within the religions gets to define what makes good and bad, and consequently whether or not any particular person gets to go to heaven. There is no way to prove or disprove the existence of these places, but it seems ridiculous to think that church leaders would get to say what you have to do to get there. Each and every one of us needs to try to live our lives as a *good* person regardless of whether or not heaven exists because it is the right thing to do, not because there might be some reward we could get for doing so.

The scientific view is that our bodies die and there is no soul that lives on. In our culture, bodies are buried or cremated. The complex molecules from the bodies are then available for the continued cycle of life. There is no evidence that a soul exists and we can't define our lives by whether or not one might exist.

It is pleasant to think that we live on in spirit through the memories of others. So, as long as there are people alive who remember us, you could say we are living through them. The best way to be remembered is to be the best person we can be and do good whenever possible, knowing that good tends to live on and multiply in others.

What is Faith?

Faith is the belief in something without any proof or even evidence. It takes faith to believe in many of today's religions, as there is no evidence that the God is real or that the Holy Books are anything but folklore and mysticism.

Many people in the world believe in one or more Gods and their belief is based on their upbringing, the culture around them and on their faith. Even if they try to use reason and logic in every other aspect of their lives, religion doesn't fall under that same scrutiny and rational thinking.

Faith also makes it almost impossible to debate religion with people. When religion doesn't fall under rational thought or logical thinking, but rather is governed by faith, you can't have a normal, open discussion about it.

What is the Bible (or Koran, or other religious book)?

These books are very special to the people who believe in them. In fact, some people believe that God wrote their Holy Book (usually through men). However, those books are not historical books – they are stories meant to teach people how to live. In the case of the Christian Bible for example, there is no historical evidence that Jesus ever existed, but the Bible tells many useful stories about Jesus. During the early years of Christianity, Catholic leaders merged the stories into a single book and edited it extensively. Then priests and clerics transcribed it with modifications and errors many times. The Catholic Church then started teaching this heavily modified version as fact.

These books are full of contradictions and, in fact, required the believers to perform horrific actions on the behalf of God; usually this meant killing others. The World Trade Center attackers were simply following their book (the Koran) that said they should go out and kill the infidels (in this case, us) and if they died in the process, they would go to heaven and have 72 virgins and could select 10 other people (when they eventually died) to go to heaven as well. Fellow believers praised and honored many of the families of the attackers here on Earth for the heroic deeds of their sons. The Christian Bible has said similar things (e.g. Abraham being willing to murder his son), but the Christians have generally become much more tolerant of other religions and more reasonable about moral behavior over time, and they ignore those older aspects of the Bible, even though they consider it the word of God.

Who created us?

Humans weren't just created; instead, we came to be what we are today through the long process of evolution. As life merges through sex, there is inevitably some variation (mutation through recombination, radiation or other source). Most of this variation is bad for survival (e.g., some of the deformities you may see in people or animals) and is not carried on to the next generations as the recipient usually doesn't survive to have children. Once in a great while, however, a variation is positive and improves the chance of survival. As these variations happen, the species changes and over millions of years, they result in new races.

The Earth has been around for about 4.6 billion years. Multiple times during its history, catastrophic changes have happened (e.g.

asteroid hits, ice ages) that wiped out much of the existing life on the planet. The life that remained continued to evolve and adapt and so new species appeared. This explains how the dinosaurs went extinct.

So, you could say that we were created by a natural process called evolution, or you could do what I sometimes do and say: "I don't know about you, but my Mom and Dad created me".

How do we know how to behave?

Many religious people believe that God and their church define morality (right and wrong), but that isn't the case. If God defined our morality, then we would be following His word through the Bible (whichever one) and that word is a violent one. These books order us to kill people who don't believe, to stone a woman to death for being raped, and practice other atrocious and immoral behavior.

In reality, we learn how to behave initially through our parents, teachers, and friends. Children who behave well are rewarded with respect and friendship and children who behave badly are punished. Later, we mostly follow laws and we learn what works and what doesn't work throughout our lives. Our culture defines what acceptable behavior is. Through much of history, slavery was an accepted practice and wasn't considered at all immoral; but today it is considered immoral and a truly horrible crime as well. There are many other examples of behavior in the past that the Church sanctioned and considered moral at the time, but today we consider these completely immoral.

Most societies have some form of *The Golden Rule*. This rule came before most modern religions, though most religions include some form of the rule. Confucius said: "What you do not wish for yourself, do not do to others".[26] In western and Christian civilization today, we recognize this behavior as the golden rule: "Do unto others as you would have others do unto you"[27], which is the way the Christians say it.

Generally, this rule says that you should treat others the same way you would want to be treated. So, if you are trying to decide if you should do something then ask yourself if that is how you would want others to behave towards you.

What are we if we are not religious?

We are Humanists because we believe in the Human race: we believe that each one of us must take responsibility for ourselves and that we all have to take responsibility for Humanity and Earth. We believe in using reason, intellect, and logic to solve problems and that we don't need to rely on faith or a God.

There are many other names that someone might call us including: Atheist, Secular, Skeptic, Heretic, Pagan, Heathen and Godless. Some of these are harsh names and don't really apply to us, and some might apply, but people don't like those names and think they are bad. Humanist is a name that we can all accept and that people recognize as being good for the Human race.

What else do Humanists believe?

We don't have a book like the Bible for Humanism, at least not yet. However, we do have the Humanist Manifesto III, which is a modern agreed-upon document describing the tenants of Humanism. The following statements come from this manifesto:

We believe that we acquire knowledge of the way the world works through the scientific method, which includes observation, prediction, experimentation, and rational analysis.

We believe that Humans are one part of nature and are the result of unguided evolutionary change over a long time.

We believe that our understanding of right and wrong come from human need and interest and that it changes with experience and knowledge.

We believe that our happiness comes from being good and doing service to other Humans.

We believe that Humans like being with others Humans and that we find happiness and meaning through friends.

How big is Humanism and how did it start?

Humanism started back in the Renaissance when scholars tried using reason and logic to explain everything, including religion. These Christians thought that religion could stand up to the scrutiny of such thought. But the term Humanist started appearing in the early 20th century and the first document describing the tenets of Humanism (the Humanist Manifesto I) was published in 1933.

It is difficult to say how many Humanists there are in the world, but some accounts that include Humanists, Atheists, Seculars and other non-religious people estimate the number to be at 1.1 billion.

What is the Scientific Method?

The scientific method is a way to try to have a reasonable idea of how the universe works. We are always accumulating knowledge and sometimes our early guesses at how things work are completely wrong. With the scientific method, we have at least some evidence that the universe works the way we are suggesting. The basic method is as follows:

1. Observe things.

2. Suggest a hypothesis that might explain what you have seen.

3. Make some predictions based upon your hypothesis.

4. Test your predictions.

5. Start over (and include the test results).

If the predictions seem to remain true during the testing, then the hypothesis attains the level of a theory, as it would appear to be a good one. A great example of this is Darwin's Theory of Evolution. He made many observations about the way the world works, especially during his travels on the Beagle (the ship he traveled on observing nature). Then he came up with a theory called Evolution that explained what he had seen. This theory also relied on research and information from previous scholars. There were parts of the theory that Darwin could not prove or even explain well at the time because he lacked the resources and technologies. Since then, others have proven every prediction his Theory of Evolution made, and so scientists no longer consider evolution a theory, but accepted fact.

Another aspect of good science is the sharing of information and ideas. As more people have access to the observations and data and can test the theories independently, the science advances even faster and we become even more accurate.

Is science ever wrong?

Science is frequently wrong, in fact, some people argue that it is always wrong because we can't know everything and all science in the past has been corrected and was therefore wrong. But, that is lame thinking. Science does its best with the data and observations it has at the time. With the scientific method, we at least have to predict results and then have positive results from testing those predictions so that the theory would appear to be correct.

On the other hand, what is the alternative? Without science and the scientific method, we would use faith and intuition to try to understand the world and that would not only be wrong, it would be completely untested and untestable.

Science and technology are improving constantly. As they improve, new data and new ways of observing are found and these can cause little changes to theories, predictions and tests, thus causing us to completely reconsider a theory. Einstein's observations and theories completely changed our understanding of physics that had stood since Newton's time. These are good changes as it means we are using the fifth step in the scientific method correctly and we are open to new ideas.

As long as we communicate and are open to new ideas and new data, we will continually be improving our understanding; this is the heart of science and the scientific method – so being wrong is just part of the process.

Should I tell people we are Humanist?

That is completely up to you. Personally, I am proud of being a Humanist and believe that Humanism offers our best hope for a sustained planet and a happy, healthy civilization. You may run into problems with some friends being surprised if you also say you don't believe in God, but that is because they were brought up in a family that has faith and does not question their religion. Humanists have not been very vocal about their beliefs or lack of beliefs, so religious people may not have heard someone say they don't believe before. My suggestion is to ask them questions about their religion and how they came to believe in God or to have faith. Question them in a reasonable and logical way. Most people have a very difficult time standing up to this since faith is not backed by reason and they can't have good, logical reasons for believing.

You can also try to explain to them that people believe many different things, some believe in their God, some in other Gods and many people don't believe in God at all, or at least think that we must live good lives independent of religion.

The one thing you don't want to do is get offensive about it. Remain open to new ideas, and try to have some empathy for them, their upbringing, and their situation. Put yourself in their shoes and try to see it from their point of view.

What troubles might I expect in school?

There are two types of troubles you might encounter in school. The first is that politics are defining what is taught in schools and religious organizations affect politics. So, school curriculums are affected by religious organizations. This means that some solid science like evolution is not being taught or it is being taught alongside creationism (sometimes called *Intelligent Design*, which is, frankly, drivel). Religious organizations attempting to proscribe history through the Bible can also influence subjects like planetary geology, astronomy, and history. Your best course of action in this case is to attempt to bring up these topics in the appropriate classes and discuss them in an open, reasonable way. This will help to enlighten everyone around you and may help the teachers to teach the subjects even when the politics say they can't.

The second issue is that some of your peers may become upset if you insist there is no God or if you say we should use reason and not faith. This may result in intense arguments and, if it really gets out of control, fights. You will need to maintain your composure and try to debate these topics reasonably and civilly.

What if I don't want to be Humanist?

What you believe and what you practice is ultimately up to you. All I would ask is that you research the possibilities, look at all the data, and come to a reasoned and reasonable decision about who you are and what your philosophies are.

What about Christian holidays like Christmas and Easter?

These holidays had their beginnings before Christianity. They are based on pagan rituals around the winter solstice (the middle of winter on the shortest day of the year) and the spring equinox (when the Sun is directly over the equator and spring is upon us). There were rituals around these events because they were so important to the farming-based communities.

The Christians took on these celebrations, renamed them, and changed them slightly to fit their religion. These Christian names are the ones we use today. Many Christians believe these are Christian holidays and so may find it odd that you celebrate them, but they haven't looked into their beginnings.

So, it doesn't matter if you are religious or not, these are cultural celebrations and there is no problem with us celebrating them.

What about our relatives or friends and their worshiping?

Frequently the best course of action here is to let them do their worshiping and be polite about it, but don't practice yourself. If they ask if you want to go to church and you don't want to, then politely say "No thank you". If they pray at the dinner table, be silent while they pray, but you don't need to pray with them or say "Amen" at the end. If they want to discuss religion, then you can decide whether you want to discuss it with them. If you feel strongly and want to have an open, honest discussion, then go right ahead.

VIII - Contemporary Issues

These issues are clearly the most subjective and the most controversial. The very nature of Humanism, just like science, allows for significant dissent and disagreement; we all just consider that part of the process. However, that leads to a wide spectrum of opinions and beliefs. Even about religion, Humanists vary from the faithful (though probably not fundamentalist) all the way to anti-religious (or anti-faith).

In the sections below, I try to present factual information and current thinking on the subject, the reasoning behind my thinking on the topic, and what Humanists generally think. Some of the topics are straightforward and it is even difficult to see why there is even a debate (e.g. evolution); others are much more complex and not at all black and white. In any case, take what I've written here, do your own research, and form your own opinion. However, keep in mind that these are contentious issues and are likely to come up in conversation. Have enough information to discuss these topics intelligently. You may also want to teach your children something about these topics as well.

Evolution

This topic, at least, is a straightforward one from a scientific and therefore humanistic viewpoint. The vast majority of scientists are very clear that evolution is accepted fact within the scientific community. Within the biologic and natural sciences, it has virtually 100% consensus. Those scientists that voice opposition or attempt to support the intelligent design stance are religious people who specifically obtained their degrees in order to counter scientific facts.

There are two main points that seem to separate the different *views* of how the Universe came to be. The first is the age of the known universe. Scientists put this at somewhere over 15 billion years. They can figure this out from data they get from very distant stars and from the rate that the universe is expanding. Of course, they may be wrong about the exact age; in fact, they may be quite wrong and new evidence may change their estimates. However, the people on the other side of this argument take the biblical approach and believe that God created the universe, *as it is*, at some point less than 10,000 years ago —science isn't *that* wrong. This ignores all the science we have with dating events from examination of the Earth and the Universe. Strict creationists argue that either God or the Devil placed all that evidence there to confuse us. God placing the evidence there makes little sense unless he doesn't want us to believe in Him; the Devil makes a little more sense and is a comical conspiracy theory[*].

The other frequently debated argument is whether life evolved through a natural selection process or by God. The hybrid between these two is that God directed the natural selection. There is no way to prove the distinction in the latter two cases, whether God had a hand in the creation of life. The argument against it, however, is that most species are simply not engineered well enough to have been done by intent. Many

---

[*] There isn't sufficient room here to cover this topic. There are many good scientific books out on the subject, or you can see www.ethicalatheist.com for a review of this and other topics.

species have odd characteristics that make no sense from an engineered or designed standpoint, but make a great deal of sense from natural selection via random mutations. This latter argument is why virtually all true biologists, geologists, anthropologists, and natural scientists are certain that *evolution without influence* is fact.

We as intelligent, reasoning beings have to use the data in front of us and the scientific method to try to understand and confirm our theories. Anything else is folly – it would be like taking a random book from history and basing your view of how the world works on that book. Michelle Goldberg said it well: "When truth loses its meaning, all manner of deceptions can be fostered"[28]. Intelligent Design is just such a deception and is a recasting of creationism. It is a sample of religious fundamentals trying to redefine *truth* through a literal interpretation of the Bible. Historically, public schools could not teach creationism because it was faith-based knowledge and not science. By recasting it as intelligent design and backing it with their own scientists, fundamentalist Christians have been able to make inroads into teaching Bible-based *truth* in public schools.

There is no real debate about evolution; any reputable scientist in the field considers it proven fact.

Abortion

This has been an ongoing debate, mostly between the religious right, and free thinkers for many decades. Most proponents of abortion point to the landmark Supreme Court ruling in 1973 of *Roe v. Wade*, which legalized abortion. However, this decision arguably just heightened the debate because the Supreme Court was ruling on what some considered a moral or even religious cause and not law (or interpretation of the constitution).

When I was a child, I had the opportunity to get involved in the movement; in fact, I toured abortion clinics and was able to see first hand the garbage cans full of baby parts, which led to my picketing abortion clinics. Being a rational thinker, I thought a great deal about the topic. From a scientific standpoint, I could see that it would be difficult to call a few-day-old fetus *life*; it is essentially a collection of cells with no feeling or nerves and isn't sustainable outside of the mother, even with the best of medical help. On the other hand, arguing that partial birth abortions are acceptable because some part of the baby is still inside of the mother seems ludicrous to me (especially after having delivered one of my own children). Logically then, the answer lies somewhere in between. After all, the argument comes down to whether or not you consider the *fetus* alive (from a religious standpoint, it would be whether it has a soul, but let's not go there). Working backwards from a fully developed fetus, I tried to come up with some point that you could say the baby is alive and there were three possibilities that I could think of. The first is when it leaves the mother's body and breaths on its own, but I had already concluded this was wrong because the baby is viable long before that and can live without the mother; the fact that it is still connected or inside shouldn't matter. The second is when conception happens, but that also didn't seem right as many babies abort naturally without the mother even knowing. Scientifically, a few undifferentiated cells do not constitute life. The third is where you might consider the baby viable. Usually this is around 24 weeks when doctors consider the baby viable (though requiring medical assistance). The problem with this last option is that it is a moving target. In the March 2007 issue of Newsweek, there was a report of a baby who was born at 21 weeks and 6 days. The shocking thing about this story is that the doctors wouldn't have even tried to save it if they knew how young it was. They made a mistake in calculating its age and thought it was 24 weeks (considered barely old enough to live). What is that magical age when a fetus can successfully become a baby if it is only separated from its mom and taken care of?

The modern neurological view is another possibility in determining when a fetus is *alive*. Harold Morowitz and James Trefil in *The Facts of Life* suggest that life contrasts with death and so measurement for the beginning of life should be determined the same way death is. Doctors generally define death as the loss of the pattern produced by a cerebral electroencephalogram (EEG).

> "If life and death are based upon the same standard of measurement, then the beginning of human life should be recognized as the time when a fetus acquires a recognizable EEG pattern. This acquisition occurs approximately 24-27 weeks after the conception of the fetus and is the basis for the neurological view of the beginning of human life."[29]

This is obviously a complex topic and even if you can settle on a definition for when life begins, you have to consider the extreme cases of incest, rape and other atrocities that might happen to a woman as well as deciding when it is acceptable to have the baby make use of the mother's body against her will. I'm a firm believer in the right to make a choice, but not when it is about taking away a life. The question becomes one of the definition of life. From a moral, but not religious standpoint, this is really the only consideration. If, at some pre-delivery point, you consider the fetus alive, then you can't just terminate it. If you don't consider it alive until it is breathing on its own, then termination pre-delivery is morally acceptable.

This has turned into such a difficult topic because there are two completely different methods for determining whether it is life[*]. The first is a religious-based one – that it obtains a soul at conception and is therefore life. The second is the scientific argument, which unfortunately isn't definitive. This argument is such a contentious one partly because the scientific argument isn't clear. Science should be factual, black and white. In this case, there isn't a clear definition other than the *when it is breathing* one, which is completely unacceptable to anyone who has seen a premature baby or a live birth.

Most Humanists today are *pro-choice*, though they would shy away from abortions in the third trimester and especially from partial birth abortions. I personally think there shouldn't be abortions after the point when a doctor can recognize an EEG pattern, but I'm a minority within the Humanist community here.

---

[*] The cultural view of when a fetus becomes a person varies around the world from conception to years after birth. A few examples are: in rural Japan, personhood is obtained when an infant utters its first cry; in Northern Ghana it occurs 7 days after birth; and for some Ayatal aborigines the child is not a "person" until it is named, which occurs 2 to 3 years after birth. See *Developmental Biology* by Scott F. Gilbert or http://8e.devbio.com/article.php?id=162.

Stem Cell Research

This is closely related to the Abortion issue because the primary argument against stem cell research is derived from the belief that *life* (or for religion the *soul*) begins at conception. From the point the egg is fertilized and cells begin to divide there is the potential for Human life. This potential of life or life itself means we must give it all of the rights that a fully delivered Human would have.

Most scientists don't consider a fetus *life* until there is brain wave activity and a heart beat, or when there is an EEG pattern (see Abortion above). This occurs somewhere around twenty-four weeks. Unfortunately, they don't rely on a single definition of life or the one the Supreme Court has agreed upon (from abortion). Instead scientists attempt to argue that the potential of stem cell research is so great that we have to continue the research; or that the medical costs of treating patients who could be cured through advances from stem cell research is far greater than the costs of not using stem cells. These arguments are materialistic or economic and do not take into account the individual's rights. They just argue that the ends justify the means, which is a dangerous and slippery argument.

Any argument to stop stem cell research has to begin with the belief that life begins at conception and any valid argument that stem cell research is worth it has to assume that it is not life at that point.

Humanists, taking the scientific stance, tend to believe life begins somewhere after conception. When exactly isn't important for this topic, but the earliest would be nine weeks, when a heartbeat can be detected.

In this case, stem cell research is not only acceptable, but also demanded by the enormous potential it offers.

Gay Rights

From a Humanistic standpoint, it is a surprise that this is still such a heated topic. Homosexuality has been around for as long as we have records. There have been various forms of it:

- Egalitarian where the partners are equal

- Gender-based where the two partners take on male or female roles

- Age-based where there is a wide discrepancy in ages

In modern western society, the egalitarian type of homosexuality is most prevalent, but in roman times, it was common and accepted for men to have homosexual relationships with young boys. The Koran also discusses young boys as a reward for men.

It is difficult to tell just how prevalent homosexuality is in modern society, mostly because of the rampant homophobia in some parts of the country. In addition, there is the difficulty in defining homosexuality – does a single homosexual experience make a person homosexual; does it require multiple experiences; or is it only when someone is exclusively homosexual, or self-identifies as homosexual? Generally, though, most research indicates that 35% to 40% of the population has had some homosexual encounter and an estimated 4% of the population claim to be exclusively homosexual. Homosexuality is also present in various animal species including a number of primates. Some report that it is well-documented behavior in more than 500 different species[30].

From a scientific standpoint, there is no evidence that a gene or genes exist that promote homosexuality. In addition, the American Psychiatric Association has been clear that "treatment attempts to change sexual orientation are ineffective"[31]. They go on to say, however, that the risks are great and can include anxiety, self-destructive behavior, depression, and suicide.

I can't specifically explain how homosexuality made it past evolution, but then attributes acquired through natural selection are extremely complex and sometimes very difficult to explain.[*] What we can say is that homosexuality is a natural phenomenon and we must give homosexuals the same rights as every other citizen, including marriage and all the rights that that includes.

However, this stance is one that tends to cause even liberal religious people to baulk. It has been a rallying force for religious people across the country, but especially in the Bible belt. Otherwise conflicting groups like Catholics, Protestants, and Mormons unite in their stance that homosexuality is evil. As Michelle Goldberg puts it:

> "Homosexuality has become *the* mobilizing passion for much of the religious right. A populist movement needs an enemy, but one reason the Christian nationalists are so strong is that they've made peace with many old foes,

---

[*] Read *Darwin's Ghost* by Steve Jones for more on this.

especially Catholics and African-Americans. Gay people have taken the place of obsolete demons."[32]

The Humanist stance on this topic is quite clear. Homosexuality is natural and is here to stay. We must provide the same rights to homosexuals that heterosexuals have and we should never be prejudiced or homophobic.

Global Warming

This is an interesting topic because it is an example of where science meets politics. It is accepted fact that the planet is warming, and warming at a significant rate that will affect us over the coming decades. Measurements over the past 100 years and proxy measurements over previous centuries and millennia confirm that the mean planetary temperature is rising at a significant rate. What is being debated in public and in politics are the specific causes of the global warming, whether it is anthropogenic (caused by Humans), and just what can be done about it.

The United Nations Framework Convention on Climate Change (UNFCCC)[33] heads an international coalition of countries and scientists that are adamant that much of the global warming is anthropogenic and that significant changes have occurred since the industrial revolution began. The Intergovernmental Panel on Climate Change (IPCC) also assesses "scientific, technical and socioeconomic information relevant for the understanding of climate change, its potential impacts and options for adaptation and mitigation."[34] The IPCC's fourth report "Climate Change 2007"[35] is due out shortly. This report includes the most definitive and comprehensive data to date that indicates much of global warming is anthropogenic. The generally accepted view is something like the following:

There are various substances that we release into the atmosphere and some of these cause warming and some cooling. The entire process is extremely complex and consequently is difficult to prove unequivocally. Nevertheless, most scientists agree that the primary cause is through the buildup of greenhouse gases – primarily carbon dioxide (CO_2), methane, and nitrous oxide – in the atmosphere. These greenhouse gases then exacerbate the normal *greenhouse effect*[*]. The worst offender is the CO_2 that we release into the atmosphere and much of this comes from the burning of fossil fuels (via internal combustion engines and coal and oil fired power plants). A significant portion of global warming is therefore the result of the high need for energy, and this need is increasing. The industrialized nations are the worst offenders, though all but the United States have taken measures to control the release of greenhouse gases. The United States and the two largest emerging countries (India and China) have 850 new coal-fired power plants planned by 2012.[36] The production of greenhouse gases from these plants eclipses the conservative limits of the Kyoto Protocol[37] (an international agreement to limit the production of greenhouse gases).

There is some debate about what we should do about global warming. This debate depends partially on the causes of the global warming, but most feel the critical path to take is to find a significant

---

[*] This is much like the effect of a green house or your car when it is in the Sun. The Sun shines through the glass and heats the interior, but the sealed green house or car contains most of that heat and so the interior heats up significantly more than it would otherwise.

source of energy for the growing demands that don't use fossil fuels or other non-renewable resource. Short term, some countries are trying to rely on Solar and Wind power more. Longer term, Nuclear Fusion appears to be the best alternative. Fusion is a safer, cleaner and more sustainable way to create energy. However, we are decades away from having energy through Nuclear Fusion generally available.

There is a small minority of scientists, however, who think that global warming is more complex and may not be anthropogenic. Nevertheless, the scientists involved directly with the studies and those going through the peer-review process are adamant that the current theories are accurate.

When science becomes political, as it is with global warming because of the far-reaching impacts, it becomes suspect. One basic tenet of science is the open, honest, challenging environment. When we stifle objection because of the political popularity of an idea, then we stifle science. It is difficult for the public to know from what we see in the news what the real global warming science is. Nevertheless, if you look at peer-reviewed information and the scientific consensus[*], there is strong agreement that global warming is anthropogenic. What are still undergoing enthusiastic debate are the possible solutions.

Most Humanists today are firm believers in anthropogenic global warming. We have to protect the planet and live in a sustainable way. Continuing to rely on non-renewable resources like fossil fuels isn't

---

[*] Try reading some at http://realclimate.org/, which is a site dedicated to the science behind the climate from "climate scientists".

sustainable and it is damaging the planet and our ability to sustain life. The two primary issues are the continuing and growing need for enormous amounts of energy and the rights of emerging countries to enjoy the same standard of living as those in industrialized countries.

One final side comment on global warming; many people seem to think that global warming means that everyone will have warmer and dryer weather. This is definitely not the case. The weather patters will shift, but a warmer average temperature means increased precipitation because more water evaporates into the atmosphere. It also is an *average*; some places may become cooler because of the shifting patterns. Don't be fooled by some cooler or wetter weather.

Neo-Atheism

This is a much more difficult topic as it includes some extremists within Humanism that aren't only less tolerant of religion, but believe we all have to become intolerant if Humanity is to survive. Granted, this isn't specifically a war against religion, it is more of a war against faith, and that is exactly why it fits into the Humanistic point of view. As Humanists, we believe in using reason, intellect, empirical data, and the scientific method to understand the world around us and to decide on how to live and behave. This is in direct opposition to faith. Some people successfully keep faith and reason separated and live their earthly lives by reason while believing that if they are moral and righteous people, then their afterlife will be taken care of (e.g. they will go to heaven). However, others believe that this very tolerance of faith is what has allowed the worst atrocities in history to occur (see *V - Religious Conflict*).

This attitude opposes pluralism, religious tolerance, and reasonable and polite behavior. On the other hand, given the 9/11 religion-based attacks and the new direction the United States is taking towards Christian Nationalism, it may very well be that we all need to become less tolerant of unreasonable behavior and beliefs not based on reason. Humanists are all over the board on this topic and it is one of continuing debate. I have heard Sam Harris (one of the main advocates of anti-faith or new atheism) called both an idiot and a savior. I personally think the advocates of this view have some valid points to make and we need to listen to them. However, their intolerance is not the correct path to take today, and for the time being, others will ostracize whoever takes that path.

Theocracy & Christian Nationalism

This may be the hottest of all of these topics and conversely the least known. It encompasses almost all of the other topics as it is the divide between Christian fundamentalists and Science in the United States that is at the root of most of these issues.

There is absolutely a concerted effort by fundamentalist Christian evangelicals to rewrite the history of the United States into one based on Christianity and subverted by secularists. They believe that the Bible should define our legal system and define truth, even when it counters scientifically established fact.

Some suggest the roots for this started prior to World War II when depression-era leaders "railed against communism, modernism, and big government"[38] and with the establishment of the anti-communistic

John Birch Society (JBS). They based their direction upon the one clause in the declaration of independence that referred to a higher being:

> "We hold these Truths to be self-evident, that all Men are created equal, that they are endowed by their Creator with certain unalienable Rights, that among these are Life, Liberty, and the Pursuit of Happiness."[39]

The reference to *their Creator* is the basis for the JBS stance that our personal rights come from God and not from Government. Eventually this stance led to *Dominionism*, a belief that it is the right and responsibility of Christianity to claim dominion over Earth and everything on it. The name comes from Genesis:

> "And God said, Let us make man in our image, after our likeness: and let them have dominion over the fish of the sea, and over the fowl of the air, and over the cattle, and over all the earth, and over every creeping thing that creepeth upon the earth."[40]

This belief leads to some harsh stances on current issues that most tolerant religious people and all Humanists counter. These include:

- Severe reactions to homosexuality with Christian activists obtaining homophobic laws that are unfair and prejudicial. Most consider them in violation of the bill of rights and the constitution. A specific intent here is to disallow sexual relations not sanctioned by the Bible; this includes consensual sex between any two partners who are not both married and heterosexual.

- Attempts to introduce the biblical concept of *Creationism* into the classroom in the guise of *Intelligent Design* backed strictly by the Bible. Previous court rulings specifically disallowed this in publicly funded classrooms because the basis of it was faith and not science.

- Contradictory stances on abortion, teen pregnancy, birth control, and AIDS. The general idea is to teach teenagers that abstinence is the only real way to protect oneself from pregnancy and disease. In teaching this though, they obfuscate and sometimes fabricate the data and they discourage the use of contraception. This is a religious stance, but is detrimental to society; some studies show that abstaining delays the first intercourse, but other forms of sex (oral and anal[*]) start earlier and when intercourse does start, it frequently does not include protection and therefore results in increased disease and teen pregnancies[†].

- Bush's faith-based initiatives are funneling millions of taxpayer dollars into unregulated and unmonitored faith-based social programs[‡]. These include:

---

[*] The Bible makes both of these proscribed as well, but they don't seem to come up in abstinence teaching. Maybe they are too sensitive, or the teachers don't see them to be as dangerous because they don't produce children.

[†] People who have made "virginity pledges" delay vaginal intercourse, but have similar rates of sexually transmitted diseases (see The April 2005 issue of *The Journal of Adolescent Health*).

[‡] These are almost exclusively for the Christian faith, which counters the stance on religious freedom in this country.

- o Teen pregnancy centers that have little or no real medical or counseling staff available and instead proselytize Christian values.

- o Christian advocacy funds that then back Christian initiatives like banning gay rights and fighting science in the classroom.

- o Replacing inner city social reform programs with faith- based programs that preach Christian beliefs, are unmonitored, and don't have professional staff.

- o Discrimination against non-Christians in programs that were previously secular and are becoming strictly Christian because of the abundance of faith-based money.

- Specific attempts to either restrict the ability of the judicial branch of government or fill it with faith-based proponents. This latter tactic has been largely successful with the Bush administration's recent appointments.

- Attempts to abolish the practice of *Separation of Church and State*. Really, this means control of the government by the church. Separation of Church and State has been a hallmark of the American system of government. There are myriad books out now by politicians proclaiming a need to get back to being a Christian nation. They want the Bible, and not empirical, rational data, to be the source for our laws.

Many of these tactics are echoes of Fascism in Nazi Germany.[*] "There are some inescapable parallels between the rhetoric of cultural purity in 1930s Germany and in our America."[41] The road to totalitarianism is paved by people that abandon truth and reasoning. They try to force others to their own ideals. As Thomas Jefferson put it:

> "History, I believe, furnishes no example of a priest-ridden people maintaining a free civil government. This marks the lowest grade of ignorance of which their civil as well as religious leaders will always avail themselves for their own purposes."[42]

Thankfully, there are emerging advocates on the rational side of this argument as well. In fact, the fastest growing *belief* segments in the country are the Christian evangelicals and the secular Humanists. This means that the masses that previously just lived their lives are joining sides to what is likely to be the next major cultural war in America. Two outstanding books that discuss Theocracy and Christian Nationalism are Michelle Goldberg's *Kingdom Coming* and Damon Linker's *Theocons*. Michelle comes from the outside of the system in the form of a political reporter and Damon comes from the inside as an editor at the center of the theoconservative world.

Consider carefully whether you want your laws and science based on empirical data with rational methods and thinking or on the Bible.

---

[*] There are various books out by holocaust victims who see the same things happening in America today as they did in Germany prior to WWII.

Even if you are someone of faith, I would hope that you separate faith from our methods of discovering how the world works.

Conclusion

Parenting has always been a challenge and it still is. Day-to-day parenting in a secular household is very similar to parenting in a religious one. Every parent, whether religious or not, faces plenty of challenges when raising children, religious or not. The differences lie in the thousands of years of rites, rituals, and practices that religious families adopt through their religion and not in any core requirement for a family to have religion. Religion does not define our morality, our behavior or our application of right and wrong. A proper and healthy upbringing is what brings about these traits.

As with everything else, the most important part of parenting is to spend the time to think about what makes a good parent and what is required to produce good children. I have heard this called *Parenting with Intent.* If you spend the time thinking about the spiritual aspects of a non-religious, healthy, happy life and apply this to parenting, much of the information in this book is apparent. It isn't rocket science, but it also isn't easy. The specifics of parenting, like how much punishment to deliver and how to handle misbehaving children are not as critical as having a plan and living up to the standards that you set for yourself.

For better and worse, however, times are changing. The religious leaders have become politicians and are attempting to turn the country into a Theocracy. There are battles raging over separation of church and state and over the influence that Christians have on our government. Extreme, fundamental religions are endangering the entire world with terrorist attacks and the day is coming when they will gain access to weapons of mass destruction. Faced with these new challenges, many otherwise quiet Humanists are becoming active and trying to show the fallacy of reliance on faith, at least in defining how we live.

I believe Humanism offers us the best hope for a sustainable and fulfilled existence.

These changes may have dramatic impacts on our society and the world. They will also have an impact on your children in the guise of arguments with other kids and idiosyncratic practices of teachers and schools (e.g. not teaching scientifically proven *evolution* or as my daughter recently told me, not being able to talk about politics in class). It is, as always, your job as parents to prepare your children the best you can and in this case, it means making sure that they have accurate, reliable, and scientifically backed information.

I hope this book has been helpful.

Resources

The International Humanist and Ethical Union: http://www.iheu.org

The American Humanist Association: http://www.americanhumanist.org

The Humanist Society: http://humanistsociety.org

The Spiritual Humanist: http://www.spiritualhumanist.info

Atheist Parents: http://www.atheistparents.org

The Brights Network: http://www.the-brights.net

The Unitarian Universalist Association http://www.uua.org

Notes

[1] Arthur Fairbanks, ed. and trans.,*The First Philosophers of Greece*

[2] Albert Rabil, Jr., *Humanism 1: An Outline*

[3] This is available various places, but try the following:
http://www.corliss-lamont.org; or
Corliss Lamont, *The Philosophy of Humanism*; or
http://www.humanists.org/hum_lamont.htm

[4] See http://en.wikipedia.org/wiki/Humanism

[5] Victor Stenger, *God – The Failed Hypothesis*

[6] Richard Dawkins, *The God Delusion;* or
http://en.wikiquote.org/wiki/The_Golden_Rule

[7] See Axelrod. R., *The Evolution of Cooperation;* or
http://plato.stanford.edu/entries/altruism-biological; or
Richard Dawkins, *The Selfish Gene*

[8] Robert Wright, *The Moral Animal*

[9] Sam Harris, *The End of Faith*

[10] Sean Curley, personal quote

[11] Archives of Disease in Childhood, April 1998, 78:293-296

[12] See http://familydoctor.org

[13] Sam Harris, *Letter to a Christian Nation*

[14] http://en.wikipedia.org/wiki/Rituals

[15] http://www.atheists.org/comingout/weddings/atheistweddings.html

[16] Michelle Goldberg, Salan Magazine, November 2005, *How the secular humanist grinch didn't steal Christmas.*

[17] The Buffalo News, November, 1984

[18] http://www.christiananswers.net/q-eden/edn-t020.html

[19] Sam Harris, *The End of Faith*

[20] Personal interview, *Anonymous*

[21] There have been a number of articles on this, but try:
Transcript of *CNN In the money*, January 28, 2006

[22] Nature, Vol. 394, No. 6691 (1998), *Leading scientists still reject God*

[23] http://1stholistic.com/Meditation/hol_meditation_healing.htm

[24] I am no expert on the Koran, so I must submit to others on the interpretation. You might try:
Inquiry & Analysis Series – No. 74: *A Muslim Debate on the Rewards of Martyrs*; or
Jihad Watch, April 5, 2004 (www.jihadwatch.org/archives/001435.php#c7737); or
Free Republic, Oct 2001, *Mohammed's View of Woman* (www.freerepublic.com);

[25] Newt Gingrich, *Rediscovering God in America: Reflections on the Role of Faith in America's History and Future*; or search on James Dobson's *Focus on the Family* site (www.family.org) for "Christian nation".

[26] See http://en.wikiquote.org/wiki/The_Golden_Rule; or
http://www.religioustolerance.org/reciproc.htm; or
http://www.familyofhumanists.org/goldenRule.html

[27] ibid

[28] Michelle Goldberg, *Kingdom Coming*

[29] See Harold Morowitz and James Trefil, *The Facts of Life*; or
http://8e.devbio.com/article.php?id=162

[30] Sara Goudarzi, LiveScience, November 2006, *Homosexual Animals Out of the Closet*

[31] See http://www.medicow.com/topics/Reparative-therapy

[32] Michelle Goldberg, *Kingdom Coming*

[33] See http://unfccc.int

[34] See http://www.ipcc.ch

[35] Download http://www.ipcc.ch/SPM2feb07.pdf

[36] See www.nuclearalliance.com/documents/EnergyInfoDigest_February2005.pdf

[37] See http://unfccc.int/resource/docs/convkp/kpeng.html

[38] Michelle Goldberg, *Kingdom Coming*

[39] The United States of America *Declaration of Independence*

[40] Genesis 1:26

[41] Michelle Goldberg, *Kingdom Coming*

[42] Andrew Lipscomb and Albert Bergh, *The Writings of Thomas Jefferson*

About the Author

Sean Curley began studying religion and philosophy at an early age, mostly from a Catholic viewpoint. While studying world religions in college, he found many had admirable and useful qualities and many had atrocious pasts and contradictory and indefensible tenets. His studies eventually led him to Humanism, and upon marrying a like-minded woman and having children, they embarked on a program of Humanist parenting. Mr. Curley has a B.S. degree in Computer Science, an M.S. degree in Engineering Management, and an M.S. degree in Space Studies. He is on the board of the Boulder International Humanist Institute; runs The Spiritual Humanist web site and blog; and is both a Humanist Celebrant (of the American Humanist Association) and an ordained Humanist Reverend (of the Church of Spiritual Humanism). He lives in Colorado with his wife and four children.

LaVergne, TN USA
13 November 2009
164016LV00004B/128/A